Contents

Have you eaten yellow foods?

Colours are all around you.

How many different colours can you see in these foods?

The Colours We Eat

Yellow Foods

Patricia Whitehouse

www.raintreepublishers.co.uk

Visit our website to find out more information about **Raintree** books.

To order:

☎ Phone 44 (0) 1865 888112

🖹 Send a fax to 44 (0) 1865 314091

💻 Visit the Raintree Bookshop at www.raintreepublishers.co.uk to browse our catalogue and order online.

First published in Great Britain by Raintree,
Halley Court, Jordan Hill, Oxford OX2 8EJ,
part of Harcourt Education.
Raintree is a registered trademark of Harcourt
Education Ltd.

© Harcourt Education Ltd 2003
First published in paperback in 2004
The moral right of the proprietor has been asserted.

Editorial: Nick Hunter and Diyan Leake
Design: Sue Emerson (HL-US) and Joanna Sapwell
(www.tipani.co.uk)
Picture Research: Amor Montes de Oca (HL-US)
and Maria Joannou
Production: Jonathan Smith

Originated by Dot Gradations
Printed and bound in China by South China
Printing Company

ISBN 1 844 21608 X (hardback)
07 06 05 04 03
10 9 8 7 6 5 4 3 2 1

ISBN 1 844 21615 2 (paperback)
08 07 06 05 04
10 9 8 7 6 5 4 3 2 1

British Library Cataloguing in Publication Data
Whitehouse, Patricia
Yellow Foods
641.3
A full catalogue record for this book is available
from the British Library.

Acknowledgements
The publisher would like to thank the following for permission to reproduce photographs: AgStock ... (... Young), 23 (pepper, Ed Young); ... ...ca pp. 12, 16R, 23 (stem); Bill ... kernels), back cover (sweetcorn); ... Photography pp. 20, 21L, 21R, ...hotos pp. 6, 18, 19 (Greg Beck), ...le, Greg Beck); Gareth Boden ...ed eggs); Heinemann Library (Michael Brosilow) pp. 4, 5, 8, 17, 22, 24; Phil Degginger pp. 11; Rick Wetherbee pp. 7, 13, 16L, 23 (vine); Visuals Unlimited p. 10 (Inga Spence).

Cover photograph of lemons, reproduced with permission of Heinemann Library (Michael Brosilow).

Every effort has been made to contact copyright holders of any material reproduced in this book. Any omissions will be rectified in subsequent printings if notice is given to the publishers.

CAUTION: Children should be supervised by an adult when handling food and kitchen utensils.

Some words are shown in bold, **like this.** You can find them in the glossary on page 23.

All of these foods are yellow.

Which ones have you eaten?

What are some yellow fruits?

Pineapples are yellow and sweet inside.

They are spiky and prickly outside.

Some melons are yellow.

Melons grow on long **vines**.

What are some other yellow foods?

This squash is yellow.

It is vegetable, but it looks like spaghetti inside!

Grapefruit grow on trees.

They look like big yellow oranges.

Have you tried these Yellow fruits?

These are lemons.

Lemons grow on trees.

These are star fruit.

When you slice them, each piece looks like a star!

Have you tried these yellow foods?

Chickpeas are small yellow seeds.

You need to cook chickpeas before you can eat them.

scrambled eggs

The **yolk** of an egg is yellow.

Have you tried **scrambled eggs**?

Have you tried these crunchy yellow foods?

Sweetcorn is crunchy.

Kernels of corn grow on corncobs.

Peppers are crunchy.

They are tasty and good for you.

Have you tried these soft yellow foods?

Ripe bananas are soft and yellow.

They grow in bunches on
tall **stems**.

Butter is soft and yellow.

It is made from milk.

What drinks are yellow?

You can make lemonade by squeezing the juice out of lemons.

Add a little sugar to make it taste sweet.

Apple juice is good for you.

It is made by pressing the juice out of apples.

Recipe: Yellow Fruit Kebab

❗ Ask an adult to help you.

Cut some pineapple, bananas and star fruit into small pieces.

Next, push some pieces of fruit onto a toothpick.

Now, eat your yummy yellow fruit **kebab**!

Quiz

Can you name these foods?

Look for the answers on page 24.

Glossary

kebab
pieces of food on a wooden or metal stick

kernels
the small, yellow seeds of sweetcorn

scrambled eggs
a food made by beating eggs while cooking them slowly

stem
the main part of a plant which grows from the ground

vine
a plant that has a long, thin stem

yolk
the yellow part of an egg

Index

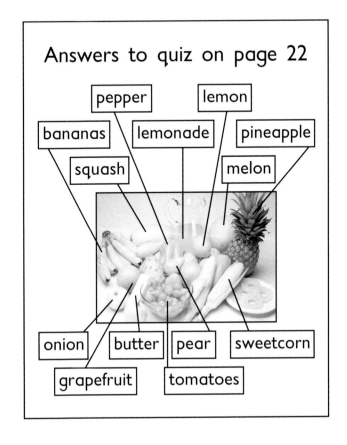

Answers to quiz on page 22

pepper

lemon

bananas

lemonade

pineapple

squash

melon

onion

butter

pear

sweetcorn

grapefruit

tomatoes